Open Letter To My Grandma

Designed
by
S.H Bando Press

www.shbandopress.com
Questions And Customer Service:
email us at contact@shbandopress.com

Disclaimer Notes

This Journal Belongs To

....

The Window by Rumi

Your body is away
from me.
but there is a
window open.
from my heart to
yours.
From this window
like the moon.
I keep sending
news secretly.

My Dear Grandma ,I want to Say

I can bear much more than you think, but I need _____

_____

_____
_____

I really wish that _____

_____

_____

_____

_____

Life without you is _____

_____

_____

_____

_____

Since you've been gone, I find it difficult to _____

_____

_____

_____

_____

_____

_____

I will be patient _____

_____

Because _____

_____

_____

_____

Now that you are gone I feel _____

_____

_____

_____

To allow these feelings room to transform into something
else, I am willing to _____

_____

_____

_____

I am ready to feel _____

_____

_____

_____

_____

_____

One way I can express this feeling in a creative way
is _____

_____

_____

_____

_____

Whenever I start to feel overwhelmed by pain, regret –
guilt, or despair, I will repeat this mantra _____

_____

_____

_____

To be more compassionate toward myself, I am willing to
try _____

_____

_____

_____

There someone else who is hurting, like _____

_____ and , _____

I could do _____

to show them I care and _____

_____

My Favourite Memories With My Grandma Is

Things That Will Always Remind Me Of My Grandma {Images – Songs – Scents _ Food – Quotes – and more}

Redemption Song by
Kevin Young

Grief might be easy
if there wasn't still
such beauty – would
be far
simpler if the silver
maple didn't thrust
its leaves into
flame

My Dear Grandma

I know I'm going to be okay because _____

_____

_____

_____

_____

A simple activity I could try in this period to make things easier is _____

_____

_____

_____

_____

I could use some more _____

_____

_____

_____

_____

I could use a little less _____

_____

_____

_____

_____

Since you are gone, I'm going to _____

_____

_____

_____

_____

My 'forward motion' plan for this month _____

_____

_____

_____

_____

_____

My 'forward motion' plan for this year _____

_____

_____

_____

_____

_____

I will depend on _____

_____

_____

_____

_____

How things have changed _____
_____
_____
_____
_____
_____

When I wake up in the morning _____
_____
_____
_____
_____
_____

When I do things like _____
_____
_____
_____

I think of you _____
_____
_____
_____

If I could tell you one thing _____
_____
_____
_____

My Favourite Memories With My Grandma Is

_____

_____
_____
_____
_____
_____
_____
_____
_____
_____
_____
_____
_____
_____
_____
_____
_____
_____
_____
_____
_____
_____
_____

Things That Will Always Remind Me Of My Grandma {Images – Songs – Scents _ Food – Quotes – and more}

"Faraway"
Poetry

After you left
nothing made
any sense: it felt like
the world was ending
yet the sun kept
rising
day after day.

My Dear Grandma

After (insert what happened) _____

_____

_____

_____

_____

I felt _____

_____

_____

I never wanted _____

_____

_____

_____

_____

_____

I'm angry that _____

_____

_____

_____

_____

I wish I could have told you _____

_____

_____

_____

_____

What I miss the most is _____

_____

_____

_____

I choose to remember you by _____

_____

_____

_____

_____

Every time I see _____

_____

_____

_____

_____ I think of you

If you were here now _____

_____

_____

_____

_____

_____

How I felt when I was around you _____

_____

_____

_____

_____

_____

My favorite thing we used to do together_____

_____

_____

_____

_____

Today I remembered _____

_____

_____

_____

_____

Our favorite places _____

_____

_____

_____

My Favourite Memories With My Grandma Is

Things That Will Always Remind Me Of My Grandma {Images – Songs – Scents _ Food – Quotes – and more}

''Faith smith''
Poetry

The sky cried with
me today.
I let the rain come
down hard
over me and felt you
in every drop.
It's as if even the
heavens
know you belong on
Earth.

My Dear Grandma

Things you taught me about myself _____

_____

_____

_____

Ten words that best describe you _____

- _____
- _____
- _____
- _____
- _____
- _____
- _____
- _____
- _____
- _____

My favorite quote that sums you up _____

_____

_____

_____

_____

_____

_____

If I could be like you in any way, I would adopt their

_____

_____

_____

_____

Your best quality _____

_____

_____

_____

_____

Your worst quality _____

_____

_____

_____

_____

Things you hated _____

_____

_____

_____

_____

_____

Things you loved _____
_____
_____
_____
_____

This quote reminds me of you _____
_____
_____
_____

_____ when you told me that
The kind things people say _____
_____
_____
_____

I will like to express my gratitude _____
_____
_____
_____
_____

My Favourite Memories With My Grandma Is

Things That Will Always Remind Me Of My Grandma {Images – Songs – Scents _ Food – Quotes – and more}

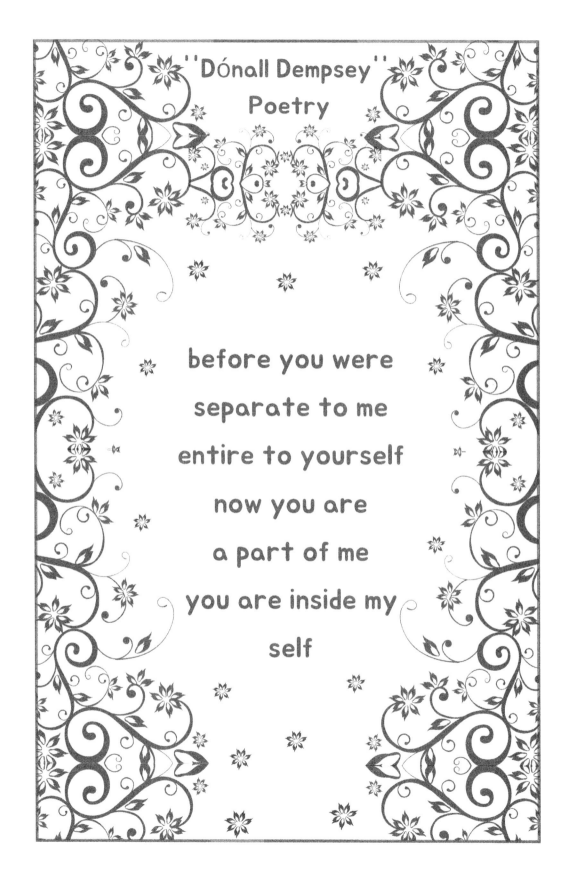

''Dónall Dempsey''
Poetry

before you were

separate to me

entire to yourself

now you are

a part of me

you are inside my

self

My Dear Grandma

If I could change one thing ,it would be _____

_____

_____

_____

_____

_____

Ten Things I've learned about myself since you passed
away _____

- _____
- _____
- _____
- _____
- _____
- _____
- _____
- _____
- _____
- _____

I am having a hard time with _____

_____

_____

_____

_____

The hardest time of day is _____

_____

_____

_____

In the last days, I have been feeling a lot of _____

_____

_____

_____

_____

How I will continue coping every day _____

_____

_____

_____

_____

My support system is _____

_____

_____

_____

_____

My support system includes too _____

- _____
- _____
- _____
- _____
- _____
- _____

A tradition that helps me remember _____

_____
_____
_____
_____

The little things that meant a lot _____

_____
_____
_____
_____
_____

I wish someone would say _____

_____
_____
_____
_____

My Favourite Memories With My Grandma Is

_____

_____

_____

_____

_____

_____

_____

_____

_____

_____

_____

_____

_____

_____

_____

_____

_____

_____

_____

_____

_____

Your last words to me

Dear Grandma, you are always in my heart

Things That Will Always Remind Me Of My Grandma {Images – Songs – Scents _ Food – Quotes – and more}

At last, give yourself time to grieve, everyone grieves differently and within their own timeframe, hopefully, some of the changes are eventual decreases in the intensity of painful feelings and longing and decreases in the length of time grief and feel overwhelming the low times aren't as low and don't last as long, As time passes and we grow, we can also have new questions and insights about our losses which change the grief we experience, just let your heart and mind heal from this traumatic experience, never judge yourself in the healing process. whenever needed, just write again freely.

	Yes	No
Do I feel much better	☐	☐
Do I recommend this journal	☐	☐
Does it deserve a good review	☐	☐

Printed in Great Britain
by Amazon

75843596R00027